T0194156

Gather Ye Sheep

Looking for and Finding the Lost Sheep

A Journey of Spiritual Growth and Testimonials of Faith

Teresa K. Guy, MS-HSA, BS MT (ASCP)

WESTBOW
PRESS®
A DIVISION OF THOMAS NELSON
& ZONDERVAN

WestBow Press books may be ordered through booksellers or by contacting:

WestBow Press
A Division of Thomas Nelson & Zondervan
1663 Liberty Drive
Bloomington, IN 47403
www.westbowpress.com
1 (866) 928-1240

ISBN: 978-1-5127-8666-8 (sc)
ISBN: 978-1-5127-8667-5 (e)

Library of Congress Control Number: 2017906936

Print information available on the last page.

WestBow Press rev. date: 05/08/2017

Acknowledgement

This book is dedicated to the Lost Sheep, to those who do not know the Lord, or the affect that He can have upon your life. May this simple book be a catalyst of change for your life for the "bigger life" that which HE has planned for you! My life is impacted every-day because of my walk with the Lord. May your life be impacted as well. I continually pray without ceasing, I sing praises to His name. I seek Him and Heaven which awaits us on the other side.

This is a gift of love for my precious family. To my precious mom, Sandra Lee Brooks, who never deserved the wrongdoings of those who hurt you. You became strong and independent. You are a precious sweet child of the father "ABBA", and I am glad and proud to call you my momma. For my sweet Grandmother who is as sweet and precious as any woman I have ever known. You are the matriarch of this whole family. You have sowed, and you have reaped the reward of a loving family: three daughters and sons-in-law, many grandchildren and great-grandchildren who love you greatly. You have brought all of this into existence- our family. Grandmother, I thank you for your courage, for your love, and for your faith in Jesus. For my sister- Kimberly, a beautiful woman who has a spirit of a wounded child- you are loved; for my brothers: Kirk Douglas Jolma, David Emerson

Bell Jr., & Justin Rowe- you matter and you are loved. Dad- "POP POP," you are loved greatly and we will always cherish your visit. Aunt Evon, I love you. You gave me the tools to get the job done, you taught me many life skills and how to survive in this old world. Aunt Birdie & Uncle Rich, you are the rock of this family. I greatly admire you and thank you for all you have done in this lifetime, and for the inspiration you gave to me for writing this book.

To my immediate family: Ernest Doyle Guy, Jr.- who first helped me with my walk with the Lord, who took the time to know me and to love me without conditions, and who also bought me my first horse and taught me how to hold-on! My husband is amazing in every way. He is the leader of our home, he works hard, and has a genuine heart. He is a God fearing and God loving man. He is my rock and my Hero. I love you, Junior, and I thank you for all that you do. My daughter, Clara Elizabeth Moon- my Jelly-bean & to Beau, my sugar-bear; you are both *beautiful* to me! I Love You both very much! I am proud of each of you. You both have an amazing relationship with our Lord and I learn from each of you every day. And now I am ready to go outside and play, to listen, and to cook dinner!

I pray for each and every member of my family. May you each find Jesus Christ and His love within your heart. May you be guided in your life by the comforter who guides us- if we ask and if we listen. Keep your eyes on the Lord, pray without ceasing, and may *joy*- fill every cell of your body.

I would like to thank Mrs. Phyllis Russelman of Clatskanie, Oregon- my home town- who prayed specifically for me when I was a young girl and who never gave up on me. And, for Tracy Ann Points and Amy Remmick who were instrumental in taking me to VBS and to church with them as a young girl, and who helped to plant the seed. May we all be able to continue planting seeds for all generations to come. I thank you both for praying for me- prayer can move mountains!

I thank Shea Morris, Shannon McMurray, and Hannah Beach- who have helped me with all computer issues and Mrs. Paula Bennett- my constant encourager and friend, Thank-you. To my church family for the support and encouragement with this project, and your prayers. A special thank-you, to the late Brother Joe Senn and His wife Ms. Brenda, the Spirit spoke through you. I have been blessed to have known such a great God fearing and God loving man. I am so proud that he gave his blessing on this project before he went to be with the Lord.

These testimonies are of great significance to me and to those who have shared them. These testimonies are like stone alters- reminders of His works. Praise be to God the Glory!

Most importantly, I thank God Almighty, Jesus Christ my Savior, and the Great Comforter- the Holy Spirit- who guides me daily- for opening my eyes to your love! I am eternally great-full for the hope you have given to me. I have learned one great truth: *It is not about the results, but it's about the obedience.*

So, I walk daily in His love, giving praises to His name, thanking Him for all things great and small, and waiting for Him to speak. I am living in the present, am great full for the past, and am hopeful for the future. Praise be to God the Glory. AMEN.

Contents

Wandering in the Desert

This writing is for the lost sheep, for those who do not know the Lord. This is for those who do not know the power of prayer. This writing is for those whom I love. This writing is about my testimony and my journey to love, joy, peace, and hope. May you find these in your life as well.

I am an ordinary person just like you. I spent forty-two years wandering and searching for answers. I searched bookshelves and churches for answers as a young adult. Back in those days, there was no Internet, Amazon, or online books in which to look for answers. I was searching for something. I needed to find what that something was. I needed to fill the empty tomb that was within me. I wanted to be filled with joy and happiness—I thought it was happiness that I could obtain from everything outside of me. I tried to fill that space, that chasm, that grand canyon of a space within me that needed filling, with anything that seemed right at the time. I wanted a family like the Waltons that I saw on TV. I wanted the happiness I saw from other families. I thought that was the happiness I was searching for! *I* tried to create both that family and that continuous joy and fulfillment. But the void continued within me. I was outwardly happy with day-to-day life, but I was not filled with joy on the inside.

I was not raised with going to church in our family. I wasn't taught the fundamentals of morals and of values. I was not raised to understand what praying was about. My brother and I were told to go to the church across the street. We were told to "get out of the house." We did go to the church. We went to Sunday school. We sang the songs. We were let out of Sunday school, and we didn't know where to go after that. Parents came to pick up their kids, and well, Kirk and I stood there. We grabbed ourselves, and we went fishing! We were not led to Christ. We were not taught about having a personal relationship with the Lord Jesus Christ, the Holy Spirit, and God. We did not really understand what it was about. We didn't get it.

I spent forty-two years wandering in the desert, searching for water. "Whoever drinks of the water that I will give him shall never thirst; but the water that I will give him will become in him a well of water springing up to eternal life" (John 4:13). I did not know—really know—that having a relationship with Jesus was interactive, or that praying meant that God would answer my prayers, or that He would hear and know my heart. I did not know He was real and that He existed. I did not have faith. I did not know. Maybe you are like that. Maybe you just have not had the opportunity to know how He can affect your life. Here is my story. May you find enlightenment or excitement in what you are about to encounter, through my experiences and that of others who have graciously shared with us their testimonies as well.

Listening for His Voice

I did not comprehend that the Bible was the *living* Word of God. To me, it was just a book with words written with a foreign pen. My Aunt Evon and Uncle Frank gave me a Bible for my birthday, which said, "To our TC, happy sixteenth birthday! Whenever you feel down and low, pick up this book and read it. It will help bring love and happiness into your heart." I did read a little bit of it and closed it; I did not feel anything. It was just a book with words on paper to me—back then. It, the book, did not bring me happiness or joy. I didn't understand the parables or what they meant. Not back then.

> And Jesus cried out again with a loud voice, and yielded up His spirit. And behold, the veil of the temple was torn in two from top to bottom; and the earth shook and the rocks were split. (Matthew 27:50–51)

The veil is the curtain that blocked the entrance to the most holy place as told in the Old Testament, where the most holy priest would sit and hear petitions of the people—and then take those petitions to God. The tearing of the veil signified that the way into God's very presence was now open to all (Hebrews 10:19–24). The fact that it tore "from top to bottom" showed that no man had split the veil. God did it. Because of this "splitting of the veil," we as believers in Jesus Christ can pray directly to the Father. Before this occurred, believers had to go to the high priest, and only he was able to go into the holy of holies in the temple and pray on their behalf. Believers can access God directly through prayer! This accessibility was only because of Jesus's sacrifice on the cross for you and for me and for all believers. We can pray directly to our Lord Jesus Christ; He hears our prayers.

Praying and listening for *His* voice is interactive. It is a learned ability, an ability that requires you to be still and to listen with your heart. It requires for you to let go of your worldly, analytical mind and to visualize and meditate on Jesus, the Word, stories of the Bible; and to trust that small voice that reveals itself—in the stillness and in the quiet. An incredible book that has helped me and may also help you in that journey is the one that I have been studying, which is *How to Hear God's Voice* by Mark and Patti Virkler. God does give you direction. God does have a plan for you. God does speak to you. God does answer our prayers. Most of the time, we do not listen; we do not know how to listen, we do not have faith; we just don't know. The Lord said to be in this world, be not of this world. The evil one dominates the world system in rebellion against God (*The MacArthur Study Bible*, p. 1582). The result of this is that evil forces dominate the earth. The Holy Spirit is here as our helper—to help Christians get through the tough times. God wants for ordinary people to willingly love Him, the One who first loved us, before we were ever born. God the Father, Jesus Christ our Savior, and the Holy Spirit are all three known as the Holy Trinity. God created it. Jesus died for our sins and our salvation, and the Holy Spirit is our earthly comforter; He is God's Holy Spirit. He is the earthly link between human kind and God the Father.

So you say because you want to doubt and you want to question—it is human nature. It is natural. It is of the flesh. *We* might ask, If there is a God, and he answers prayer, then why do bad things happen to good people? We—I say *we* because I have lived it, I have questioned, I have doubted, I am a sinner—"for all have sinned and fall short of the glory of God" (Romans 3:23). Well, that is of this world. In layman's terms, we live on the earth; we are not in heaven. We don't know things of the heavenly realm. Only God knows all things. We are human, and we are flesh. The Lord says to be *in* the world, and be *not of* the world. Good things happen, and bad things happen—**to all people**.

But it is how we deal with the adversity in our lives that makes the difference. Everything happens for a reason. God has a plan for each and every one: "For I know the plans I have for you ... They are plans for good ... to give you a future and a hope" (Jeremiah 29:11). We don't have all the answers to all the questions. We don't know everything this side of heaven. I believe that sometimes things happen to make us stronger, or maybe to help us to be a more compassionate person toward other people who might be going through the same situation. You see, God is a God of love. His character is that of a loving God. He cares. He wants the best for each one of us. His Word says so. I just believe. I just have to not question everything to the point of driving it into the ground. You say to me, Why do you not question His existence? Well, I will tell you. There are a lot of things that have happened in my life to where I do not need to question. I believe in God the Father. I believe in the Holy Spirit. I believe His holy Word, the Bible. And most of all, I believe that Jesus Christ is the Son of the living God and that heaven is a real place. And I don't even want to mention hell, but I do believe it is a real place too.

Hearing the Holy Spirit for the First Time

Here's my testimony. Here is why I believe in the Holy Trinity. Here is where my true faith began. Here is my truth. What follows are detailed accounts of how God has entered my life and the lives of some friends of mine. God has created change that is visible for me to see with my eyes and the effects of which I can feel in my heart. So I can share with you how He works when you believe in Him and when you rely upon Him and when you trust in Him. When you cry out to Him—He will answer.

These testimonies are real. These testimonies are not made up for your reading pleasure. These accounts are for you to see visibly how God works, how He can be trusted, and how He can be relied upon. He increases *faith* in His people. "For whatever is born of God overcomes the world; and this is the victory that has overcome the world—our faith" (1 John 5:4).

It has been my mission for several years now to share my testimonies, my life events in which God has intervened—and other people's testimonies, so as to be obedient—to share the God of my life with others. My God is the same God whom Moses prayed to and spoke with on the mountain. He is the same God yesterday, today, and tomorrow. These accounts are not make-believe, they are not made up, they are not fairy tales. They are for real. These accounts happened. And I give all glory and praise to the Almighty God, to our Savior Jesus Christ, and to the Holy Spirit. So it is with obedience that I "go to the lost sheep ... and preach 'the kingdom of Heaven is near'" (Matthew 10:5–7). My precious and obedient preacher, Brother Joe Senn, and his lovely wife, Miss Brenda, have encouraged me through the Word of Jesus Christ to go out to the lost sheep and share the Word—to go out and *be* the church. The Lord said to me, "Have patience, lean unto me, and have great faith." May the lost sheep who are wandering in the darkness find *the* Light who is Jesus Christ.

My Testimony

As I was driving my car to Monroe, Louisiana, on October 28, 2004, at about 5:00 a.m. with my daughter Clara, I looked down to grab my cup of coffee. I looked up, and the fog had moved in and was so thick I could not see the road! I screamed, "Where did the road go?" I literally could not see a thing. It was still dark. The fog was so terribly thick. I heard a voice say within my being, *Turn the wheel a quarter of a turn.* I simultaneously thought, *I don't know what a quarter of a turn is and what direction. We must be right out of the woods. We must be where the little curve in the road is.* This all happened so quickly! My hands on the steering wheel moved counterclockwise as if someone took ahold of my hands and the steering wheel and turned it! We then went down an embankment, and the car came to a stop.

I wasn't sure where we were. I looked at Clara through the rearview mirror above me, and she was fine. We were both fine. At that instant, I didn't know the gravity of what had just happened because the fog was still so thick. After a few minutes, I opened the car door. The fog seemed to have lifted slightly, and I looked around to see cars up on the highway. We were in a cow pasture on the opposite side of the highway. I felt dazed at what happened. I called 911, and the woman who answered the phone knew my husband who worked for the DOTD highway department, and she phoned him after getting a police car to where I was. It didn't seem like it took very long for the police and for my husband, Doyle, to arrive. The police officer asked me what happened, and Doyle saw I was pretty shaken up, and we spoke. But I just could not stop thinking about what had happened.

The voice told me to turn my wheel "a quarter of a turn." It was not an audible voice that you hear with your ears but a voice from within my being. After some investigation of the scene, Doyle told me-I could not have done with my car what I did with my eyes wide open on a clear day! My car went across four lanes of highway traffic without hitting one vehicle, which is a miracle in and of itself, at the end of the Crowville-Baskin road intersection (Praise be to God the glory!). Not only that, but my car went through five strands of barbed-wire fencing and between a telephone pole and a t-post, knocking off only my passenger side-view mirror. The car had scratches from the front of the hood all the way up and over the top of the car down the back side from the barbed-wire fence. Can you believe that we actually drove my car out of that cow pasture that day and drove it back to Crowville—nine miles from the accident? If the steering wheel had not have made the quarter of a turn, we would have surely hit the telephone-pole head on driving approximately fifty miles an hour. In retrospect, I stand amazed at what could have happened! We could have been killed that day!

Clara and I were surely saved that day by the Holy Spirit, who intervened in our behalf. I didn't hear an audible voice outside of my head; Clara Beth did not hear any voice. It was the Holy Spirit speaking to me within my being. I felt a presence upon my hands, guiding my hands in the turn; otherwise, how would I have done what needed to be done so quickly without hesitation? I am so grateful that we did not hit someone else that day! I am so glad that we didn't hit the telephone pole, and that Clara nor I had any negative side effects from the accident that day. I think about it every time I pass that intersection. I give thanks to God, the Lord Jesus, and the Holy Spirit for guiding me every step of the way and for loving us enough to be with us when things could have turned out so incredibly different. I believe that this is why I am led to share my testimony with you—because I was once a person who did not believe in the power of the Lord Jesus Christ, the Holy Spirit, or in the power of prayer, nor did I know anything about the love of God. But that has all changed now.

Getting to where I am now spiritually has taken a lifetime, so it seems. Like I said earlier, I spent forty-two years in the desert, wandering like the Israelites before they reached the Promised Land. The Lord spoke to me. His Word has come alive to me. The Bible is not just a book to me anymore. I have learned that *His* Word—the Bible—is the living Word of God. I have seen His Word answer the questions I have had, and His Word has helped to strengthen my faith. The Bible is filled with many words to help me feel joyful and happy. By the way, those feelings don't get obtained by acquiring things or by trying to make things seem happy or joyful from the outside. They are the inside effects of continuous closeness that one has with the Lord being in your heart and having a relationship with Jesus Christ, our Savior, and the Holy Spirit. I made a commitment on October 10, 2006, with my husband as we were both baptized and became newborn Christians to live with Christ in our hearts. That doesn't mean that we became perfect. But what that does mean is that we have the Lord Jesus Christ and the Holy Spirit within us. We have help when we need it. We have a spiritual guide to continually help us with our lives on this earth. We do have fruits of the Spirit—love, joy, peace, and hope—that does surpass all understanding.

When we pray, God hears our prayers. As we get closer to Him, He gets closer to us. As we put more and more faith in Him, we start to understand His love for us. We start to feel the fruits of the Spirit within us—love, joy, peace, and hope (only a few of the fruits of the Spirit)—which are those things we experience when we have Jesus Christ in our hearts and our lives. He reveals to us our true potential and our gifts that we already possess in order to glorify His name.

In the Beginning—Enlightenment at the Slumber Party

Back when I was a teenager, as teenagers do, we had a slumber party and played games. We played a game whereby everyone sat in a circle, and two in the middle held hands and said some sort of hocus-pocus-type stuff. My best friend Tracy Ann and I were in the middle. The pencil stood straight up and pushed against our hands and moved our clasped hands across the center of where we were sitting. Well, it was the start of the enlightenment for me. It was real—it was not a joke. My eyes were wide open, and I was witnessing something that was real. No strings were attached, and no one was playing a joke. We were starting to get into something that we all knew we needed to stay away from. In my mind, I thought, *If there are certainly evil spirits, then there must be good spirits.* I started to understand that there is much more to just living on this old earth than meets the eye. That was when I started to feel the need to understand about what the Bible was about and what spiritual fulfilment was all about. I didn't really seem to get very far at that time in my life, but the seed of curiosity had been planted. It just took many, many years for that seed to get planted in fertile soil to get watered and to grow.

I have seen my prayers answered by crying out to the Lord. I have literally cried out to the Lord for his help. I cried out to the Lord as I was driving home from work one day. I squalled and yelled in my car. I hit the dashboard and squalled until I came to a stop and just sat in quietness in the driveway at my home (definition of *squalled* or *squalling* in the South is when we cry out in agony and are completely consumed with grief). It was at that same period of time when my husband and I had fasted for two weeks. When we fasted, we did not watch TV for two weeks, and I committed to not drinking coffee. We committed that time for family time and for worshipping the Lord. I relied on the Lord, and He heard me. After those two weeks of fasting and crying out to Him, my prayer was answered. My daughter, who was living with her father at the time, came back to live with me.

Crying Out to the Lord

Another time, I cried out to the Lord; I squalled in total fright and humility. I knelt at the foot of the cross and prayed like no other time in my life. I had put my house up for sale in West Monroe, Louisiana. I told the Lord that I had enough money in the bank for exactly two house payments for that house, and after that, I didn't know what I would do. I asked the Lord for the house to sell immediately. I squalled and squalled because I was scared. I felt alone. I told a friend what I was going through, and she said to just call upon the Lord, and so I did. I really did. I said unto the Lord, "Please help me to know what having faith really means. Help me to rely on God for my strength. Oh God! My Savior!" I was so scared. I prayed for a month. I cried out to the Lord nonstop. Once the real estate agent took charge of selling my house, it took seven days on the official real estate market for it to sell. God is good! God answers prayers! It took exactly two house payments, and the house was sold. God works miracles! No matter what obstacle lies in the way—He can move a mountain! I thank you God for answering my prayer. I thank you, God, for building up my faith! I know what it means to trust in the Lord. I give all thanks and glory to God. If I ever waiver on whether I believe in God or his power, I just reflect back on this one time of my life, and I am quickly reminded of how I was completely in his hands. I waiver no more. I am completely convinced of His love and power.

Reflecting back to when I was in college, I had no idea what I wanted to study, or how my life's journey would start, or where I would end up. I changed my major officially five times. I was discouraged, and I felt isolated. I didn't have a clear path like most of the other young adults I knew. I struggled in class and getting through college. It was not an easy path for me, but when I graduated from high school, I didn't have any other direction or clue what my life's journey was going to be about. While in Anchorage, Alaska, at the University of Alaska, Anchorage, I do remember crying out to the Lord (I just wanted help; I didn't really *get it* that he was helping me all along) for direction and for a plan.

I somehow—and I say that because it happened out of the blue—started talking with a girl whom I had met, and she invited me to her class to check it out and see if I would be interested in her line of study. I did go to her class, and I saw microscopes, and she told me about looking at blood under the microscope and how interesting that was. She was in a medical technician (two-year) program. I became interested and changed my major from nursing to medical technology. Two years later, I found myself in Clarksville, Tennessee, at Austin Peay State University where I enrolled in a four-year program and then graduated with a bachelor's degree in medical technology. It is amazing to me where the spark came from to head in this direction of study and where I ended up. I used to kick myself in the hind end for changing my major from nursing to medical technology, but now I see I am right where I was meant to be. It is amazing to me how God has orchestrated the events of my life to where I am today. I was led in the right direction, and I am happy with the career choice I have ended up with. I didn't know anything about this field of study; I never met anyone in this line of work. I was completely unaware of what laboratory work was, what being a medical technician was, and even what working in the hospital laboratory would mean. So for me, ending up in this field of work is amazing, and the fact that I am pretty good at it and I still like it after twenty years of doing what I do is amazing. And I thank God for His direction and *answered prayers.*

God Answers Prayers!

Many years ago in 2005, I quit my job in Monroe, Louisiana, as the director of education at one of the local two-year colleges on faith that I would be able to find another job immediately. I felt a calm and a peace about the decision. I was not worried. I knew that I would be going back to my college degree and educational training and experience as a medical technologist. I had absolutely no fret or worry with entering back into the medical field after five years of working in the two-year college setting. The Lord helped me to go right back to working in the hospital laboratory setting. I went in and went right to work. It was like I had never left laboratory testing—I went right in and did my job. I didn't realize it at the time, but looking back, I see that the hand of the Lord was upon me the whole time. With no fear, with no hesitation, with everything I had, and with His help, I was able to restart my career. What a blessing. Praise be to God the glory!

One day, I was at work, and I was toting my heavy "big" Bible. I noted to myself (not out loud to anyone) that I was really in need of a small Bible, one that I could carry in my purse. My "big" Bible was heavy and too large to tote around in my purse. The next day, when I got to work, my coworker told me that there was a Bible on the table in the break room, and I could have it. Confused, I went to the break room and looked to see what she was talking about. The evening before, a Gideon, who was being obedient to the Lord's direction, came to the lab and dropped off a small white Bible. It was the size of my hand. The Bible had the books of the New Testament and Psalm and Proverbs in it. I picked it up, and tears ran down my cheeks. My prayer was answered. I didn't speak this need out loud. I know it was divine intervention. Thanks be to God the glory. "Delight yourself in the Lord; And He will give you the desires of your heart. Commit your way to the Lord, trust also in Him, and He will do it" (Psalm 37:4–5).

In November of 2014, I had a situation arise that I wasn't sure how we were going to handle. It all unfolds this way: I had a horse that needed to be picked up at one horse trainer's ranch due to a sudden change of events that were out of my control. I was thinking that my husband would have to travel the sixteen-hour trip by himself and go retrieve the horse himself because I was working and the kids were in school. We didn't really want to do this, but we didn't know what we were going to do. Meanwhile, my neighbor became friends with a sweet woman named Ms. Loretta due to a friendly smile at a horse show. She would become a friend to us all. Due in part to her many connections, she spoke about her personal horse trainer and friend and the fact that he may be able to help me out since he lived close to where my horse needed to be picked up—out in Texas. Her trainer was indeed able to arrange to have my horse picked up and taken to his ranch for proper training. The way God orchestrated that whole event was truly a miracle! It all worked out! I give God all the glory. I was in a bind, and I was in need. God is good!

Journal Entries

What follows are a few pages out of my personal journal. These accounts are real. They are to be used to help illustrate the power of prayer and obedience and to show how God hears and answers us when we pray to him. You don't see God with your eyes. You see the effects of God with your heart, with your mind, and with your soul.

In January of 2013, I started having words appear in my thoughts and in my mind. I didn't know what was going on at the time. For weeks, a word kept coming into my mind, and I didn't know the word, but I kept saying it in my mind. I liked the word. I didn't know what it meant, but I realized I would have to look it up one day. One night at work, the word popped into my mind again, and we were not busy, so I got on the Internet and looked it up. The word was *proclivity*. Shortly thereafter, I kept having these words appear in my mind, and I would continue to look them up and try to understand what was going on. I questioned what all this was with these words popping up in my head. One night, as I was looking these words up, it was revealed to me through further reading and studying that these words were being given to me by the Holy Spirit. I decided to get a journal and start writing all these words down and their definitions. I figured that it may surely mean something for me to learn from one day. I started the year off saying I wanted to increase in my faith. It was the start of a journey that has me still yearning for more. I have also learned that I can have an interactive conversation with God, and that answers do come, and that communication is possible for all believers. Not only does God hear us by prayer or by petition, but He also speaks to us or answers us. Here are some words I will share with you that were revealed to me at the beginning of that year. I figured that I was being given these words for a reason, for me to learn and grow. The words and their meanings are as follows:

1. *Proclivity.* Having an inclination or predisposition toward something, having a natural tendency to like something, having an affinity toward something
2. *Edification.* Intellectual, moral, spiritual enlightenment or improvement—such as being "spiritually uplifting"
3. *Exhortation.* Encouragement such as a speech or written passage intended to persuade, inspire, or encourage, such that it may be "urgent advice or recommendations"
4. *Parakletos.* Advocate when in reference to Jesus Christ, comforter or helper when referring to the Holy Spirit
5. *Absalom* (spirit). For example, in reference to a person's camouflaged bitterness, unresolved offenses, disappointments, and anger and stubbornness; someone who gets "offended at everything, no matter how minor"

I was an example of the above description. I prayed that I would be able to forgive completely, and I prayed for a change within myself as these words were revealed to me and as these words kept revealing themselves unto me.

These words would come to my mind as I was riding my horse; usually, it would be after a long trail ride. It was a peaceful time. It was a very rewarding time for me. Even now, I keep trying to recreate those times—it hasn't happened in a long time, but maybe it will happen once again one day down the road. I do pray the words start coming once again. I will start trail riding again soon and getting closer to the Lord, and maybe the closeness and peace I once knew will infiltrate my being as it once did.

On the night of June 14, I said, "God, this conversation seems to be going only one way. I want more of you. I don't know if you love me or if my prayers are being heard." After working all night, I came home and got into bed for my nap around 9:00 a.m., June 15. During my sleep, I heard music and a song. I knew the song well and thought to myself (while I was sleeping), *I need to remember this*, and I said, "Oh, I won't forget that song. I know that song and have known it all my life." The music was as if a radio was on in the next room. I tell you I heard it playing. When I did finally wake up several hours later, I had forgotten the song but remembered hearing music. I asked God to remind me of the song, and instantly I remembered. Here is what I heard: "I love you more than I can say / I'll love you twice as much tomorrow / Yeah, I love you more than I can say." God answered my prayer—yes, He loves me! Can you believe that? Yes, *He* does answer prayer!

Also, in June of my journal notes, a dear friend was on his deathbed, and he was close to death. But when I went to visit him, the song "I've been redeemed by the blood of the Lamb" was so strong in my mind I sang it out loud and proud just for him. He was an old oil-field tough talker, and not so mild-mannered back in the old days, but he was far removed from those old days. He was remarried, and he had given his heart and life to the Lord. He loved for all the right reasons— his sweet wife, his daughter, his grandkids, the pastor, and his friends. He had been redeemed by the blood of the Lamb. He said he wasn't afraid; he said he was ready. He had been forgiven. We can take comfort in that.

In August 2013, I wrote in my journal:

> I cast my cares upon the Lord. I had a lot coming up in my life, so it seemed … possibly going to the day shift, wanting to sell my house in West Monroe, stuff that was on my heart and my mind at the time. August 19, I got a word and scripture from the Lord and looked it up and wrote it down. Deuteronomy 2:7: "For the Lord your God has blessed you in all that you have done; He has known your wanderings through this great wilderness. These forty years the Lord your God has been with you; you have not lacked a thing" (*The MacArthur Study Bible* 2006). All I can say is, praise be to God the glory!

October 5, 2013, I read a new book out on the market because it caught my eye. The title of the book was *Waking up in Heaven* by Crystal McVea and Alex Tresniowski. I love true stories and especially stories where people learned something on their spiritual journey and share it with the world. The three key points she wanted to convey to the reader are these: (1) God said tell them I love them. (2) She states emphatically that she learned from God that Jesus really did sacrifice himself on the cross so that when we are face-to-face with

God, we know we have been saved. (3) Jesus is the reason we have hope for eternal life. That was an amazing journey. Those are well worth writing down!

Over the next three months in my journal, I kept receiving scriptural passages, and so I looked them up and wrote them down. Here are just a few of what were written:

December 2, 2013

> Continually meditate upon and be directed by the commandments that God has given. Continually bind them to your hand and forehead. (Deuteronomy 6:8)

December 10, 2013

> For now we really live, if you stand firm in the Lord. (1 Thessalonians 3:8)

> But since we are of the day, let us be sober, having put on the breastplate of faith and love, and as a helmet, the hope of salvation. (1 Thessalonians 5:8)

In church, we were reminded to always "put on the full armor of God, so that you will be able to stand firm against the schemes of the devil" (Ephesians 6:11). Look those up! Read about the full armor.

January 13, 2014

> And we know that God causes all things to work together for good to those who love

God, to those who are called according to His purpose. (Romans 8:28)

Those who love the Spirit love God. Those who are in the Spirit can understand the words of God.

Those who do not operate in the Spirit do not understand the word of God. (1 Corinthians 1:18–2:14)

People who are "of the earth" do not allow their minds (spirits) to dig deeper for the Lord for spiritual advancement—to be humble, quiet, and soft in allowing the Spirit of Jesus to dwell and speak. The "worldly" are too loud, too caught up in the world. We need to allow the soft inner voice to speak. Turn off the music, turn off the TV, and tune out the static and the chaos. Enjoy peace. Enjoy the quiet. Listen and hear.

On January 20, 2014, I wrote what I heard God speaking to me, softly saying, *Have great faith.* I also prayed that day that the Lord would help me not be double-minded. I have had a yearning to move back to my hometown of Clatskanie, Oregon, where my childhood friends are and where I would be closer to my family. I had a dream of that, but in order to not tear my family apart, I have to let that go. My husband says he will not move from his hometown. And so to keep the peace and be logical, I have to stop yearning for such a drastic change in our lives. I want my husband and myself to be together, and I do not want anything to tear us apart. I love living here. I love our home; it is a blessing. I would miss our beautiful roses, which we have been growing out front, and we just planted apple trees and pear trees, and I want to see them produce fruit one day. We have great jobs and a great life. It is so illogical for me to have such a double mind and yearn for something that is so out of the realm of our possibility and not at all what we need anyway. I asked God to help me to not be double-minded.

Psalm 23—Revealed

On February 11, 2014, I was studying Psalm 23. I wanted to do more than read it. I wanted to really get to the depth of it. We were doing a Bible study in my women's class, and we were digging into the Word. The Word comes alive to you when you read it with the Holy Spirit guiding you. It opens up, as it did for me that day when I read the passage once again, but with a new heart and a new mind. Here's what I have gleaned from the Word.

The Lord is my guide. I follow after him. He is the all-knowing. He knows what I need and supplies my needs. He makes me feel safe. Even the timid deer cannot go to the water and drink for fear of predators—but *He* makes me safe. I do not need to fear with Him in my life. "For God hath not given us a spirit of fear; but of power, and of love, and of a sound mind" (2 Timothy 1:7). When I am afraid and/or when I don't know what to do in life, I pray. He hears me. He knows my heart. He speaks to me. He makes the way peaceful. He helps my mind and soul to be still and know He is Lord. When I go through hard times, or I am upset—He is with me. I am not alone. His Word helps me to know what is right and what is wrong. Oh, I am not perfect, but I can turn to Him for help when I stumble on a rock on the path. He knows I am human and cannot be perfect—that is the humanness we have to deal with on this earth.

He prepares a table before me; I have never gone hungry. He feeds even the hungry sparrow. His Holy Spirit guides me and fills me with joy. The fruits of the Spirit are love, joy, peace, and hope. I feel those. If you don't feel those, then I know a man who can make that happen for you too—Jesus. He says he has a mansion awaiting me one day, and I fully believe that. So I don't need to worry on this side of heaven. He is my reward. He wants me to be content with what he has given to me. I will dwell in the house of the Lord forever because I believe in His Son, and I believe His Word.

That day, I didn't really know what the rod and the staff were all about, so the whole passage took on a new meaning for me. The rod is a corrector. It is meant to keep us in line, like the shepherd keeps the sheep in line. He also uses the rod to keep predators away from his sheep. The rod is used as a protector. Additionally, God's commandments are like a rod, which helps us humans to know right from wrong and keep us in line. His staff pulls us back to Him when we stray from Him, just like the shepherd would pull the sheep back toward him if they wandered too far from him. God's Spirit pulls us back toward Him as he puts thoughts of doing what is right into our minds. From the beginning, God imprints on every heart a conscience, the knowledge of right and wrong (Romans 2:15). The Holy Spirit opens our eyes to the truths, to the meanings of the Bible.

Parables: A Clear Understanding

I have friends who have blessed my life and do not mind helping me to learn by sharing what they have gotten from the Word. This is what Bible study is all about. Small Sunday school classes and small Bible studies are for growing the new babe in Christ, or even the seasoned Christian. What a true blessing to be able to share the Word and to see the "light" of Jesus go on and see the excitement of understanding the Word. I'm excited to get deeper into the Word! That's *Bible* study!

Parables are short stories that Jesus spoke of to help relay a message for better understanding of God's love for the people—the people of even today. Some people say or believe that the parable is just a story and leave it at that. Some people read the parable and say, "I do not understand," and walk away. And yet there are some people who persevere and keep studying the Bible, attending Sunday school, and are able to eventually *get* understanding through the revelation that the Holy Spirit places upon each and every believer. Preachers, teachers, friends, neighbors, loved ones, etc., are people who can help enlighten those who are not in understanding of the Word. I have been going to church regularly for twelve years now, and I am so excited when a part of the Holy Word comes to life for me! I sure don't know all there is to know about the

Holy Word, the Bible, but I have learned a few things on this journey, and I continually learn.

In Luke chapter 2, Jesus unfolds three parables: the parable of the lost son, the parable of the lost coin, and the parable of the lost sheep. In the parable of the lost son, the younger son says to his father, "Father, give me the share of the estate that falls to me." So the father gives him his share. The son then goes on his merry way, spending money foolishly and living the wild life. And then he finds himself broke and alone. He gets a meager job of feeding pigs and comes to his senses. He says, "How many of my father's hired men have more than enough bread, but I am dying here with hunger!" So he decides it is best to go back to his dad and get in the "right" with him and tell him how sorry he is for not listening to his good counsel. The son says, "Father, I have sinned against heaven and in your sight. I am no longer worthy to be called your son. Make me as one of your hired men." But here is how the parable goes: While the son is still a long way off, his father sees him and feels compassion for him. The father says, "Quickly, bring out the best robe and put it on him, and put a ring on his hand and sandals on his feet. Bring the fattened calf and let us eat and celebrate because my son is coming home! For this son of mine was dead and has come to life again. He was lost and has been found."

The son, in the beginning, didn't want a relationship with his dad; he just wanted his blessings. He wanted the reward of the money. But being foolish, he squandered it all quickly. He had what he wanted. What he didn't know was that he had all he needed and wanted all along—with his *father*. If he just stayed there with his father, he would have already had all the money he could possibly have wanted or needed. But he was unaware of his riches. He was chasing after riches and glory when he already had it to begin with. The son didn't want the relationship; he just wanted his reward.

But I tell you that the same is true with God. He wants a relationship with me and with you. He wants us to be filled with the Spirit, to enjoy the riches that he provides: wisdom, love, joy, and peace, to name a few. We are dead in Christ if we are striking it out on our own, if we think we know better than *He* does. So when we turn to Christ, when we have Him in our hearts, when we pray to Him and learn to expect our prayers to be heard—and wait for his answer—when we as *Christians* praise and worship the Lord, that is when we have a relationship with Him, who *is* the Father. We are then seeking our eternal riches and blessings of heaven. That is when we are no longer lost; that is when we are *found.* In the parable above, the "father" is God, and the lost son is representative of any lost soul or unbeliever in Christ Jesus.

God rejoices when He sees us coming closer to Him. God is a God of Love. He is a God of peace and joy. God's character is one in which he *always* wants what is best for you. He always has your back. He is our spiritual Father. A father does not want bad things to happen to his son or daughter, just as our Heavenly Father does not want anything bad to happen to his children. He loves you. He loves you. He loves you. Remember that.

The parable of the lost coin goes like this in Luke 15:8:

> What woman, if she has ten silver coins and loses one coin, does not light a lamp and sweep the house and search carefully until she finds it? When she has found it, she calls together her friends and neighbors, saying, "Rejoice

with me, for I have found the coin which I
have lost!"

Verse 10 continues saying, "In the same way, I tell you,
there is joy in the presence of the angels of God over one
sinner who repents."

I have always read the parables for just exactly what they
say—I thought the woman lost a coin! But in a sermon one
day, the lightbulb went on for me as Brother Joe explained
that the coin is representative of a lost child of the woman. If
a woman has a child who is "lost," then she will do what she
needs to do in order to turn on the light of Jesus in that child's
life. Jesus is the Light of the world. The woman will clean the
household and the child's life by sweeping out the negative or
bad things that are in the child's room or in the child's life.
The woman is like the Father of Heaven. The woman doesn't
want any of her children to be lost in the world, and neither
does God want any of His children to be lost but rather found.

And the parable of the lost sheep is similar to the
other two.

> Jesus says, "What man among you, if he has a
> hundred sheep and has lost one of them, does
> not leave the ninety-nine in the open pasture
> and go after the one which is lost until he
> finds it? When he has found it, he lays it on his
> shoulders ... Rejoice with me, for I have found
> my sheep which was lost! ... I tell you that in
> the same way, there will be more rejoicing in
> heaven over one sinner who repents than over
> ninety-nine righteous persons who need no
> repentance."

A person is considered lost if he or she does not have Jesus Christ as their personal Savior. Are you lost? Do you feel an emptiness within yourself that you cannot seem to get rid of? If you do have emptiness, if you have loneliness, lack of joy; if you have negative thoughts, bad dreams, or even worse, you may be lost in the world—take heart. You can be found. You can find joy. You can get rid of the negativity and the bad demons. It's not over; the race is not complete. You still have time to enjoy those positive things.

March 2, 2014, I was asked in my Bible study class, "So what's your relationship with Jesus?" I had been asked that question before. A long time ago, I would have answered. "Really? I don't have a relationship with Jesus." But on this occasion, I was prepared, and surely I said, "It's a two-way relationship. It is active. And it is real." I pray, and sometimes when I am quiet, I hear a small voice, and sometimes I wake up with clarity or have an answer. Sometimes, when I ask God even for something as menial as where is that glove, a picture in my mind will appear like the closet or the bathroom or on top of the washer. And there I will go to search, and there I will find what I am looking for. I thank God then and there for the answer. What a *great* and *awesome* God He is!

March 27, 2014, I had an incident happen to me, and what was revealed to me more than once—through the preacher at church and by a television preacher all in the same week—the very center of the Bible is a passage. In the very center of that passage, which is the very most center of the Bible, it reads "It is better to take refuge in the Lord than to trust in man" (Psalm 118:8). I took great comfort in that because a dear friend hurt me badly. I was cut to the quick. I was wounded emotionally. But I was made stronger. A few months later, I found myself in a very similar situation as the previous one. I was cut to the quick and hurt on a personal level two different times in the same week. I had to dust myself off, get back up, and allow God to work in my life. By trusting in Him, I had a *better* situation occur than what was previously in place to begin with—Isn't God *good*! It was God who orchestrated the events that took place, and only he could have made it turn out as good as it did! Praise be to God the glory. (Reference to the horse experience I spoke about in God Answers Prayer!)

On May 25, I asked God for assurance that he was still with me. I cried out to him because I wasn't hearing Him like I once had. I had not been as close to Him as I once was. I was in a quandary about some things, so I cried out to the Lord. On the May 27, I heard him speak softly, *I am with you now. Remember that the foal born on Easter Sunday morning is my gift to you, to know that I am God. I am with you always.* My mare was not supposed to have her baby until May, so we were not expecting a baby that beautiful twentieth day of April early Easter Sunday morning. We had a surprise, and we were so excited! My son Beau slid all the way across the kitchen floor in his socks in excitement. We were both excited! We hurried to get our boots and jackets on and headed out the door behind my husband and across the back pasture to see that playful little white foal that was born in the wee hours of the morning. Yes, God is *good*!

In my journal, I write down my questions, my prayers, and what is on my mind. I wait to see if I will hear the Lord speak to me. I wait in the stillness and focus on Jesus. I place my mind on Jesus. I try to keep all other outside distractions or worldly stuff out of my mind. It is hard to do. I find that when I wake up before the kids get up, before the TV goes on, before the sun pops out (about 4:30 to 5:30 a.m.), I can find the stillness and quietness I need to write in my journal and be able to pray. Sometimes it is after everyone goes to work and goes off to school that I can find the quietness at the house to where I can be still before the Lord.

Keep a journal for yourself. You will be amazed at what fills those pages! They will be reminders of the amazing things God does for you. Even the Israelites were instructed to build memorials of stone that would remind their ancestors of the miracles God had done for them. Same thing with your journal. It will be a reminder of the words spoken to you through the Holy Spirit and a reminder of the many ways God will affect your life.

Oh, there are times where I have prayed for things, and I didn't hear anything from Jesus, and I don't get everything I want. God knows what we want and what we need. He knows *His* great plan. He has all the answers. Sometimes we make it hard for him to do his work because we try to make what we want happen rather than taking no for an answer—because we think we know what is best. But He may have an even *greater* plan! I wish I would have known about God, His Son, Jesus, and the Holy Spirit a long time ago! But He has made what I have done work out for his glory. I know that He has spoken to me before, but I did not listen. I was hardheaded and stubborn, and quite frankly, I didn't know— and was scared. I thought I knew what I was doing, but God knew what His great plan was. He has made *sweet lemonade* out of the mess I created. I can only thank God for what he has done for me through His Son, Jesus.

The Holy Spirit Speaks
at Delhi Lake

Just before my son was born, an old credit card bill had resurfaced after many years that it had been forgotten. It was a great sum of money, and I didn't know how I was going to get it paid with a baby only months away from being born. All the stress just seemed to be pushing in on me. I worked hard at the Rayville hospital that Christmas holiday. We had a coworker who quit, so I was covering her shift. I hated working the midnight shift back then! It was not appealing to me. However, I found that my paycheck that holiday consisted of (1) my regular pay, (2) overtime pay, (3) third-shift differential, and (4) I got holiday pay on top of all that in a matter of just two weeks. The following paycheck was an answer to prayer! The totaled amount of that paycheck covered the whole credit card bill. It was a staggering amount of money. I have never seen another paycheck the likes of what that one was. It was a miracle. It was an answer to prayer!

In the summer of 2014, after our boat ride at Delhi Lake, we decided to walk over to the public beach. My son was playing in the water—he loves it. I asked him not to get out past his knees. We had no plans of playing in the water, and we had no towels or extra clothes. We were just planning on going for a ride in the boat with his daddy, and that was it. Beau (five years old at the time) wanted to play farther out and farther out in the water. I hollered to him and signaled for him to come back toward me, but he did not comply. He kept walking farther away from me. As I sat there, the Holy Spirit spoke to me clearly and said, *He thinks he can swim to the buoy.*

A split second later, I saw him bobble down beneath the water, and I sprinted toward him as fast as I could. A young girl walked toward him, and as he was headed back beneath the water for the second time, she reached him with her hand, and I was close behind. I grabbed that wide-eyed boy! He was gasping for air, his blue eyes wide open and scared. He clung to me. I just held him tight as we walked closer to the shallows of the shoreline. I knelt down in the shallow water and noticed it was warm. I didn't want for my son to be scared of the water was why I stayed in the water. I asked him what he was doing. He said to me, "I thought I could swim to the buoy."

At that time, he did not know how to swim, and he did not have on his life jacket! Since then, we have started swimming lessons, and we never go near water without a life jacket! At the very mention of this situation, Beau will tear up. He remembers the feeling of being scared. I remember the exact moment the Holy Spirit spoke to me. My son might have died that day. That girl who walked toward him and reached him seconds before I did told me that she thought he could swim, and she thought he was just playing—until she saw me screaming as I was running toward him. Here is a huge thank-you to that sweet girl, who doesn't even know that she saved a life that day. She was a hero. I thank the Holy Spirit for intervening in my life for the second time, with a life-threatening situation. The first time was when Clara and I ran off the road, and the second time was when Beau almost drowned. The Holy Spirit is my hero! Second only to Jesus Christ, my Savior, who died on the cross for my sins and for my salvation.

The Lord is present with you when you have Him in your life. He says to me all the time, *I am with you always.* I ask Him, "Are you there?" He says, *I am.* It is when I need help in scary situations that He is there. But always remember, He is there within you always.

How Does He Speak to You?

How do you get the Holy Spirit to be with you? You may be saying, I want that! I want to have assurance of going to heaven when I depart from this earth. You might be thinking, How do I have a relationship with the Lord? How do I get started? Well, I will share with you exactly what the Virklers have laid out because it is so good. I have so many quotes from the Bible. I have read so many passages that I just cannot rewrite them all. My whole Bible is filled with underlines and highlighter marks, but that's part of the fun—reading and rereading scripture, becoming familiar with the books of the Bible and where they are located. My six-year-old is learning the books of the Bible now; I am learning with him! I am such a beginner, a babe in the Word. I have been for the past ten years! The Word of the Lord is a living Word. The *Bible* is the living Word of God. It speaks to you and to me if we ask and search and look and read. The Holy Spirit helps to bring us understanding.

Before sin entered, God walked in the cool of the day with Adam and Eve. Once sin entered, God was not able to flow freely within their lives. He was separated from them by their sin. God is a God of love and compassion, so he sent his one and only Son, Jesus, in the form of a man to be the sacrifice for the sin that separated God from mankind. As written by Mark and Patty Virkler (pg. 229):

> By entering the world as a man, God was able to take the sins of the entire world upon his shoulders and pay the penalty of this separation by allowing His Son Jesus Christ to be separated from Him for a moment in time. That is why Jesus cried out while dying on the cross, "My God, My God, why have you forsaken me?" However, in forsaking His Son for a moment in time, God restored the opportunity for you and for me to return to the experience of the Garden of Eden, and once again, have fellowship with Almighty God.

Our relationship with God can be assured with the following steps as written by the Virklers:

1. *Acknowledge that you are a sinner.* "For all have sinned and fall short of the glory of God" (Romans 3:23).
2. *Repent.* "Repent, then, and return to God, so that your sins may be wiped out" (Acts 3:19). Ask God to forgive you of your sins. Turn away and do them no more.
3. *Confess.* "If you confess with your mouth, 'Jesus is Lord,' and believe in your heart that God raised Him from the dead, you will be saved" (Romans 10:9).
4. *Forsake.* "Let the wicked forsake his way and the evil man his thoughts. Let him turn to the Lord ... for He will freely pardon" (Isaiah 55:7). *Turn away from your old sinful nature.* Turn to that of (1) loving your neighbor as you would love yourself, and (2) loving

the Lord with all of your heart, and your mind, and your soul.

5. *Believe.* "For God so loved the world that He gave His one and only Son, that whoever believes in Him shall not parish but have eternal life" (John 3:16).

6. *Receive.* "He came to that which was His own, but His own did not receive Him. Yet to all who received Him, to those who believed in His name, He gave the right to become children of God" (John 1:11–12).

We have this promise:

> If the Spirit of HIM who raised Jesus from the dead dwells in you, He who raised Christ Jesus from the dead will also give life to your mortal bodies through His Spirit who indwells you. (Romans 8:11)

When the Lord or Holy Spirit speaks to you, it may be in the form of a picture or a thought that pops into your mind. It may be a word or thought that comes to you in an instant. For example, in the middle of the night, I may wake up, and a picture of a relative or friend I have not spoken to in a long time comes to my mind. I immediately pray for them. I don't know what it is going on, but God does. I pray for God's intervention to take place. I pray for their well-being and safety and love. When God calls, it may be a constant urging, or something that keeps nudging at you, or something that keeps coming to your mind and you keep thinking about.

God's character is one of an always loving and caring God. He would never put bad thoughts into your mind. God's urging and nudging is always of love and for a good outcome. Anything other than that is not of God. I repeat—anything other than what is good or what is right or what is true or trustworthy or is not of love is not from God. So determine if the thought(s) are of good character, from the Lord or not. Sift through the rubbish and select the good things and reject the bad thoughts. Always know that God is a God of love. His concern is for your well-being. God would never allow or want evil to enter our minds—that is not of God. God only wants what is honorable, what is true, and what is trustworthy for His children because that is who *He* is. He is a God of love and peace. His holy Word says so! Remember, God always has your back. He wants you to do well. He wants you to be happy. He wants his children to love Him freely.

If you want to have the assurance right now that you have the Holy Spirit within you and that you will see heaven on the other side, then you can, right now, offer a prayer such as the following to either get you started or to renew your relationship with the Lord (Virkler, pp. 230–231):

> God, I come to you in the name of your Son, the Lord Jesus Christ. I acknowledge that I have sinned and fallen short of your ways. I repent of my sin and ask that the blood of Jesus Christ cleanse me of all of my sins. I receive this cleansing even now as you weep over my soul. I confess with my mouth that Jesus Christ is the Son of God and the Lord of my life. I invite you, Jesus, to have first place in my heart and my life. I believe God raised Jesus from the dead, and that He is alive in my heart today. I forsake any evil ways and thoughts which I have harbored and this day turn my life over to Jesus. I ask, Jesus, that you fill my

heart and my mind with your ways and your thoughts and that you begin a transforming work from within my heart and my spirit. By believing in Jesus and His life within me, I am assured a place in heaven with God. I receive eternal life this day. Thank You, Lord Jesus Christ. I yield myself right now to the moving of the Holy Spirit within my spirit. Holy Spirit, please make this very real in my heart and let me sense you within me. May you seal this prayer this day in the name of the Lord Jesus Christ, Amen.

DATE SPOKEN: _____.

Write down date and time you spoke this prayer. Get a Bible out and write it in your Bible, or go get yourself a good study Bible. I have the *MacArthur Study Bible*, among others. I like the red-lettered Bibles too. The red wording represents the words spoken by the Lord Jesus Christ or God. Please read the full content of the following in your Bible, where Jesus was, asked and He answered,

The two most important commandments are:

1. To love the Lord your God with all your heart, with all of your soul and with all of your mind, and 2. To love your neighbor as you would love yourself (Matthew 22:37–39)

Beloved, let us love one another, for love is from God; and everyone who loves is born of God and knows God. The one who does not love does not know God, for God is love. (1 John 4:7–8)

No one has seen God at any time; if we love one another, God abides in us, and His love is perfected in us. (1 John 4:12)

The Romans' Road to Salvation

- "I am not ashamed of the gospel [the Bible]. Because it is God's power for salvation." (Romans 1:16)
- "For all have sinned and fall short of the glory of God" (Romans 3:23)
- "For the wages of sin is death. But the gift of God is eternal life." (Romans 6:23)
- "While we were still sinners Christ dies for us!" (Romans 5:8)
- "If you confess with your mouth 'Jesus is Lord,' And believe in your heart that God raised Him from the dead, you will be saved. (Romans 10:9)
- "Everyone who calls on the name of the Lord will be saved." (Romans 10:13)

You might be thinking, Yeah, Teresa, but I have sinned real big. God could not love a sinner such as myself. And yet I say to you, there is not one sin as great as cannot be forgiven by God. He is a *great* and *mighty* God! He loves you as much as any parent can love his or her child. It is written in Romans 8:38,

> For I am convinced that neither death, nor life, nor angels, nor principalities, nor things

> present, nor things to come, nor powers, nor
> height, nor depth, nor any other created thing,
> will be able to separate us from the love of
> God, which is in Christ Jesus our Lord.

Brother Joe Senn had said for months, "God loves you! God loves you! God loves you!" Whenever it is inspired from the Holy Spirit and it is in succession three times, you better believe it is important to understand. So just remember what I was once told; it is of importance: When you have asked God to forgive you of sin—He is ready to forgive. He casts it out into the depths of the ocean. It is forgotten. God says he forgives you, if you ask. He doesn't hand to you a fishing pole in hopes that you would go fishing and bring it up to him again. He has forgiven you. Let it go. You have not created a sin that is new to him. He has been around a long time. He knows of no sin that you can create in your life that He has not seen before. You can ask for His forgiveness, and you can turn from that sin and not do it again and be reborn as a new Christ like child in the eyes of God.

Does that mean you will be perfect? No. Does that mean you will never sin again? Probably not. What that does mean, though, is this: now you have the Holy Spirit to guide you and to help you to not want to sin and to help you strive to do better. You also have Jesus Christ, our Lord, to turn to and ask for help from. And when we are face-to-face with God Almighty on the day of judgment, Jesus will be there as the intercessor to help justify our sins—because He was the one who *won* our salvation. We have a hope and a future with Jesus Christ. We have the assurance of eternity with Him. For these reasons, I am filled with humility and gratitude for my Savior who assures me salvation and a place in heaven.

"For I consider that the sufferings of the present time are not worthy to be compared with the glory that is to be revealed to us" (Romans 8:18). I don't know about you, but I am excited for the everlasting life that we will have in glory with the Lord! I find great joy in my life. I don't need loud music, alcohol, drugs, sex, fireworks, chocolate, food, or any other thing to create joy in my life. The Lord will help you find great joy in what you have. He will help you be content with all that you already have.

The Lord works through us and in us each and every day. I see God in my life as I wake up and enjoy a sky filled with His glory! We saw an *amazing* sunrise the other day. The sky was filled with colors of purple, orange, yellow, and blue! It was unbelievable. We all commented on it. It was beautiful, and it made me think of *His* presence. He is what I think about in most beautiful settings. I heard it once said that the sun's rays that stream through the trees and radiate upon the earth that you can see—and you somehow feel God's presence—are, in fact, His eyelashes hitting the earth. He is present in everyday things. He is present when I hear the birds sing in the trees in the day and when I see the beauty in the stars at night. God's presence is not just in the beauty I see around me but in the atmosphere of the people and in my own actions and self-control. I feel His presence when I am speaking to patients at the hospital, or when I can help in even a small situation by getting a chair for a patients' loved one who is already struggling with heartache. It is in the smallest of actions that the Lord is present, when you can diffuse a situation or spark a smile or a hug.

Jesus is within each of us who believe in Him. He's not *only* there for us in times of trouble. He is there to help us love deeper and laugh with even more gusto! He helps us live more robustly! He helps us enjoy life even more so! What I know is that love is an amazing thing. God is love, so we can infer that he is pretty amazing! If you have God in your life, then you have the Holy Spirit in your life. The fruits (or rewards) of the Spirit are listed in Galatians 5:22, which are love, joy, peace, patience, kindness, goodness, faithfulness, gentleness, and self-control.

I have heard it said in the past that a person would not believe in God because he could not "see" God. Well, I have seen the effects of God. Just like you cannot see the wind but you can see the effects of a 60 mph straight-line wind! I have "seen" perfect strangers helping the homeless.

We saw a nation help those in New York after the 9/11 disaster and after Hurricane Katrina hit New Orleans. We have seen the hearts of a nation reach out to others in times of disaster, in times of need. The manifestation of love toward others in need is an example of God in motion. It could be as simple as a church handing out sandwiches to farmworkers, just to show love; or a bunch of neighbors coming together to help out another neighbor when his truck hauling corn turned over and spilled his corn out all over the road an in a ditch. Those fellow farmers/neighbors pulled together all their resources to help gather up all that corn so he wouldn't lose the crop and his income. All those folks came together to help out a neighbor, and they spent many hours getting all that corn up. That's an example of the love of God.

Making sandwiches for some elderly widows and taking those sandwiches to those little widow ladies in obedience to the promptings of the Holy Spirit is a form of the love of God. It is also expressed when an over-the-road truck driver leaves his tools and some paper towels in order for an old man to fix his broken-down truck at a truck stop. That truck driver had to get on his way before the old man could make it back with his needed part to fix the broken-down truck, and so the big-truck driver just left behind those needed tools and paper towels. He didn't have to do that. It was a blessing to the old man. God's love is evident in the everyday stuff up to the big stuff—God's love is everywhere.

I have, in fact, gone on a mission trip to Houston, Texas, myself to help feed the homeless. We have mission workers in our church who travel to all parts of the USA and overseas to speak about the goodness of God; to take food, clothes, and blankets; and to carry the good news of Jesus Christ to people who are lost. These are the effects of God with which you can see with your eyes, but it starts out as a heart thing. God changes the heart! The Holy Spirit changes the heart, and Jesus is the reason we have access to God and his heart changing! You don't believe me? Just look at those people who have Jesus in their hearts—they have Joy, they have peace at night when they lie down to sleep, and they have love for other people.

I have heard people say, Why don't those people who travel overseas just witness and give to the people here in the United States? We have plenty of needy people here! They say this with disgust in their voice. Well, those missionaries have to go overseas in order to witness to those who are "hungry" for the Lord so they themselves can gain confidence in order to witness and give to the lost in the United States—because the majority of Americans are *not* hungry for the Lord! Those missionaries go overseas so they can gain confidence within themselves to speak about Jesus Christ our Savior to others. It is a scary thing to do, especially when people do not want what you are trying to offer!

The United States, for the most part, has lost its appetite for the Lord. We have wandered so far away from the Lord that we slam the door in the faces of those trying to share His love. It is not easy to witness or share love to a dying nation that is slowly turning itself away from Him. However, you can see the workings of God if you look hard enough. God is a God of love, so if you see love being shared, then you are seeing His workings through people here on earth. Yes, there is evil. You can find it anywhere you look. You don't have to travel far. Just hit the remote, and you can see all kinds of nasty filth on the TV, in the news, on regular TV, on the Internet, on the cable channels, etc. Yes, there is even evil in the form of false witnesses for Jesus Christ. There are false teachers and false witnesses. You have to be aware that these exist and are out there. You have to discern between true leaders and false leaders. Those who teach from the holy Word are true leaders.

As you get to know the Holy Word of God and as you grow in the Lord, you will be able to know what is true as you lean on the holy Word of God. As your church leader (preacher, pastor, etc.) and your Sunday school leaders teach out of the Bible, you will become familiar with true doctrine and that which is from God. Additionally, you have to let go of always being so negative. You have to find the good. You have to find the love because it is there where you will find Jesus Christ, our Savior. You have to ask yourself the question, Am I a part of a positive factor in my life and in my community, or do I cast out negativity and gloom? Do I cast love off me, or do I continue to see everything negatively? Do I affect those in my life, in my home, and in my community in a positive manner?

While I was working one day, a fella asked me as I was walking past the nurses' station to a patient's room, "Why are you so happy all the time?" I just blurted out, "Because I have the Holy Spirit in me," and I kept walking. That is the assured confidence you can have when you have been saved and when you have *joy* in your life—a joy that is there in spite your upbringing, in spite your past, in spite your past sins (which you have cast into the ocean, so don't go fishing!), and in spite of *you*; a joy that the Holy Spirit has placed there. Do you have that *joy*?

One person said to me, "I don't want to quit having fun, Teresa." And that was why she could not accept the Lord as her Savior. The Holy Spirit allows you to have more fun, allows you to enjoy life *more* fully and *more* aware than ever before, so what fun are you missing out on? I personally have the assurance that (1) when I am in need or in trouble, I can count on Him being there. I get down on my knees and see what He can do! (2) I can count on His promise to love me no matter what! I am not alone, and I am loved. His Word says so. And (3) He is alive. He hears my prayers, and He answers my prayers. Not always do I get what I pray for, but if I pray and it is in His will, then my prayer will be a yes.

The following testimonials are real events. These testimonies are for your benefit, to see how God directly affects our lives in real situations. May you see the glory in each of the following testimonials. Each of these testimonials is for someone out there. Maybe you have wondered where that voice came from, or maybe you have seen circumstances happen and have been in awe at how the situation came together—God's hand was in it.

> Our life is eternal and that's God's gift to
> us. And, this life is our gift to God.

Additional Testimonies- Lives Affected

Mrs. Paula Bennett

This testimony began on March 16, 1992. My brother was a very special person. He never met a stranger. His personality was very special, and best of all, he loved the Lord with all of his heart. My brother was working in Roanoke, Alabama, with contract phone work. There he met a young lady, and they became friends. She was a divorced mom with two little boys. My brother was her hope of a better life for them. As my brother was taking the young lady home after a movie on Sunday night, they were followed by her ex-husband. The scene that unfolded was my brother being shot with a shotgun and killed. Meanwhile, the ex-husband proceeded to reload his gun in order to shoot his ex-wife, who was able to get away. In the middle of the night, I received the phone call telling me of the incident. Two days later, my sister, her husband, and I made the trip to Roanoke, Alabama. A very hard trip! We were to meet at the phone station that day because things were still very uneasy. As we were headed to the phone station that morning, we read my brother's favorite Bible verses, which he read every day before going to work:

> For this reason I say to you, do not worry about your life, as to what you will eat; nor for your body, as to what you will put on. (Luke 12: 22)

> But seek His kingdom, and these things will be added to you. (Luke 12:31)

That morning, we got to meet the young lady who was his girlfriend. Her name was Sonya, the same name as my oldest daughter, whom my brother was very close to. God was working here! The meeting with Sonya was pleasant. She told us that she worried all the time and that my brother had underlined scripture for her and was teaching her about not worrying all the time: Luke 12:22 and 31. That was my sign from God that my brother was where he was supposed to be. God was with us on that trip!

Funeral arrangements had been made, which totaled $900. Once getting to my brother's personal belongings, we found that he had the exact amount of $900 in his wallet. God was working here! The funeral expenses were actually paid by the Alabama Crime Victims fund—God was working here! We still had to drive my brother's truck home to Louisiana. That truck had bullet holes all over it! There were cops everywhere, pulling vehicles over all the way from Alabama to Louisiana. We got that truck home with not one incident or being pulled over! God is good! We go back in "2017" before the parole board again.

Mrs. Sandi Brooks[1]

Being a very young eighteen-year-old, I was already married and had a one-year-old daughter, and I was pregnant again. Our second baby girl was born two and a half months too early. This was in 1965, and not much was done with preemie babies at that time. I went into labor and was told to go to another hospital because that one didn't care for patients without insurance or had no way to pay. We found a facility, and that was where I delivered a beautiful baby girl. Our little girl didn't make it. She lived for forty-eight hours but was just two and a half pounds. I got pregnant right away and had another preemie child. In a period of three and a half years, I had three children. I was also going through a divorce and traveled from Oregon to Montana to care for my grandmother who just had surgery. I was trying to be a good mother to my children and a nursemaid for my grandmother. I was worn out and depressed with what was going on in my life.

It was a beautiful spring day in Great Falls, Montana, and my grandfather discovered the baby not breathing. She was six months old at the time. How could God take one more child from me? Now I was really depressed, lonely, and still trying to care for my three-year-old daughter and my grandmother. No one could be so cruel and unloving. I was devastated and blamed God for my hurt. I cried and yelled. Then out of nowhere, like a slap in the head, I was told right then and there that *He* would care for the children, would care for them as only He can. I was in no shape to give them what they all needed. It was a blessing and a miracle. It took

---

[1] Mrs. Sandy Brooks is also my precious momma, who also is as "great" as a superhero to her grandkids in Louisiana.

many months for me to realize the loss was a salvation. Later in my life, I was blessed with a good husband and two more beautiful babies. I was ready to go on, and we provided love, shelter, and cared for them with all our heart.

> For I know the plans I have for you ... They are plans
> for good ... to give you a future and a hope.
> —Jeremiah 29:11.

Mrs. Pamela Thorson Nicodem

I had been struggling with discouragement. One evening last week, I fell on my knees and surrendered my sorrow to God—because, at the time, I couldn't look on the bright side of things for nothing. Two days later, I heard a sermon on thankfulness, so I began to pray that God would give me a thankful heart. I listed ten things to be thankful for, and even though I made them silly, God still honored my prayers for a thankful heart. The next day, I added ten more things to the list. Now, after being verbally attacked last night by someone whom I had never dreamed would do so and facing the trauma of it, I had to pray even harder to regain that thankful heart. But the coolest news of all—I woke up this morning, and I began right away to think of all the things I was thankful for! Now, that was awesome. God answered my prayer. All I have to do is put it together—Lord + joy = strength.

Do not sorrow ... for the Joy of the Lord is my strength.
—Nehemiah 8:10

Mrs. Bonnie Parker

I know this seems hard to believe, but *believe*! I accepted God into my heart at the age of eight. I wanted a tree from God, a banana tree. I prayed nightly for months for this tree from God. One morning, I awoke with a tree from God! Not a banana tree but a red maple tree. It was growing at one end of our trailer house. It was full grown with grass growing all around it. There was no new dirt; it was not freshly planted by man. My parents were so amazed at my faith!

We have to believe in God and continue to pray every day for what we want and be patient and wait on God's timing. He will answer our prayers and give to us what we want on his timing and in the form He knows best.

Mrs. Bonnie Parker

There was a two-year-old patient of mine who recently turned two. Her momma brought her into the doctor's office. Her momma said she had been fussy and just not herself. This little girl woke up from naps complaining of her head hurting. We did CT scans of her head, and the scan showed that she had a serious brain tumor. We called the parents to come back to the clinic for us to tell them the news. They immediately flew to Memphis, Tennessee, to St. Jude's Children's Hospital. The seven-hour surgery was scheduled for Tuesday, and the surgeons told them the goal was to remove 50 percent of the tumor, as that was all they could extract safely.

After the surgery was complete, the surgeon and the staff came out with tears in their eyes and shared the news with the parents. They were able to remove 100 percent of the tumor, and they exclaimed that they had never felt such peace in the room as during this surgery. The amazing thing about the surgery was that the surgeon who performed this procedure had done over 150 surgeries on tumors of this exact type. He was the *best* surgeon for this procedure! The oncologist who was assigned for this case was again the number one doctor in the hospital to work on this two-year-old little girl. It was revealed that no chemotherapy would be needed as the tumor was in stage two, which was good if you have cancer! God truly had his hand upon this little girl and her family. All the procedures and outcomes have gone very smoothly.

> Be anxious for nothing, but in everything by prayer
> let your requests be made known to God. And the
> peace of God which surpasses all comprehension, will
> guard your hearts and your minds in Christ Jesus.
> —Philippians 4:5–7

Mrs. Bonnie Parker

My daughter Mandy was so sick off and on for over two years. She would run a fever of 105 degrees for a few days and have a white blood cell count (WBC) of 20,000 to 38,000 (5,000–10,000 is the normal WBC). She was in and out of hospitals in New Orleans, Louisiana; Houston, Texas; and Monroe, Louisiana. All the tests kept coming back negative. Finally, with high fever again, I lay on the floor facedown in my room, and I prayed! I told God that I knew Mandy was his and only mine for a short while on this earth. I didn't want her to suffer anymore. I told Him that if he wanted her, to please take her so she wouldn't have to keep going through this every few months. Shortly after that, I felt so much peace. And Mandy has not had any more problems with high fever and high white blood cell counts.

> After you have suffered for a little while, the God of all
> grace, who called you to His eternal glory in Christ,
> will himself perfect, confirm, strengthen, and establish
> you. To Him be dominion forever and ever. Amen.
> —1 Peter 5:10–11

Mrs. Shannon Greer Burge

Our journey began a few years ago going to doctors' offices, trying everything we could do to get pregnant, but to no avail. After a miscarriage, we decided that the best thing we could do was to leave it in the hands of God.

Four years ago, in a Sunday night service, a message was being preached about the fact that God can do anything, and the question was asked if anyone had anything they wanted God to do for them. I'm sure, like us, everyone raised their hands. As the message continued, the man of God stopped at our pew and asked my husband what it was that he wanted God to do for him. My husband told him that he wanted a child, and as I sat there beside him, tears began to stream down my face because I was thinking of the same thing. He prayed for both of us that night for God to give us the desires of our heart.

We left church that night excited! We got out the baby-name book, and we began picking out names. We were expecting to get pregnant, but you see, sometimes we tend to put God in a box because we think things should happen a certain way, but God's ways and thoughts are so much higher than ours. Remember, that was on Sunday. Friday morning, I went to work as usual. I went to my office and began my day. We were located right off Highway 15, and you could hear the traffic steady passing by outside. Every few seconds, someone would honk as they passed by. I sat there a little bit, thinking, *Okay, if someone honks again, I'm getting up to see what is going on.* It wasn't ten seconds when there was another honk! So I got up and went to the window. Directly across the street from where I worked were the sweetest ladies holding up signs proclaiming that it was Foster/Adoption Month and had a phone number to call. I thought, *God, if you have to hold a literal sign up for me to get this—then okay!* Those ladies could have been on any corner in downtown Winnsboro, Louisiana, but God put them right across from where I worked that day. I called the phone number and began the process.

We went into the classes strictly for adoption, but they talked us into being certified for both adoption and foster care. By the end of the course, we decided that we would try foster parenting. The first two boys whom we had in our home were eighteen months and four years old. We put our whole heart into those boys. One day, without warning, I got a phone call from the caseworker saying the judge was sending them home and that she would be there in an hour to pick them up. That was one of the hardest things that we had to go through, and I told my husband that I didn't think I could do that anymore. Days passed by, along with a lot of tears. The house was just too quiet. We had to have more kids! They soon called us for a brother and sister whom we knew up front would not be with us for long. It ended up helping us work past the disappointment and sorrow we felt previously.

On a Friday evening, I got a call from another foster parent asking if I still wanted a baby. *"Yes, of course!"* was my answer. She received a call from a caseworker about a five-week-old baby who came into care that day. I remember sitting in the Wal-Mart parking lot writing down the phone number she gave to me. When I called the number, it was already after 5:00 p.m., so it went to voice mail. When I called the other foster parent back, she told me the baby had been placed. All I could do was say, "God, you know!" I couldn't help but have a heavy heart because it seemed so close and yet so far away. The next morning, the same caseworker called me back and wanted to know if we were still interested in that baby. The previous placement did not work out—imagine that! Little baby Jared came to live with us that evening. And it was a new beginning.

He had a rough start in his life. He had to go through drug withdrawals. He was born with a hole in his heart. He had seizures and impaired vision. But to look at him now, you wouldn't have a clue where he began. It was three and a half years later when our adoption became final in August. Oh, I didn't tell you, from the time that we had that church service until the day Jared joined our family was exactly nine months. I have no doubt that God planted a seed that night, and though my labor was not a normal birth experience, it was as God wanted it to be.

I cannot tell you that this experience has been an easy one, but the blessings far outweigh the bad, and I wouldn't change one thing.

Ask and it will be given to you; seek and you
will find; knock and it will be opened to you. For
everyone who asks receives, and he who seeks
finds, and to him who knocks it will be opened.
—Matthew 7:7–8

Teresa K. Guy, MS-HSA, BS MT (ASCP)

Sergeant Ernest "Doyle" Guy Jr.[2]

During a military training mission, we needed to tread water to where we needed to be. Several hours into this training exercise of treading water and carrying heavy packs and weapons, it was about six hours in total of being in the water. We could see the Humvees where we were to end the mission and be done. We gathered all our rucksacks together to make somewhat of a floating raft of sorts. My comrade "Ski" found some high ground and took a break. Willie Henry got himself in a bind and was having trouble, so I helped him with his equipment by taking his weapon and strapping it to myself. We were all in full combat dress, which included rucksacks and weapons. It can get tough treading water for a long time, especially if you take on more than your own equipment. I got tired myself, but I helped get Willie Henry to the bank. Then I went back out to where Ski and the others had made the makeshift raft. I said to "VanTassel," "Dude, I'm tired." We had M60s and M16s and all the rounds strapped to us, making it all that heavier and much harder and harder to stay afloat as we were getting more and more tired. The rule is, you do not drop your weapons or leave them behind. We made sure the equipment was intact.

I told VanTassel I was going to lie back a second and take a break. He said okay. I remember lying my head back, kind of trying to do the float thing. I remember going under the water very briefly. I remember the water going over my eyes, and I could see the surface of the water, and I was just a couple of inches down. I felt like I was so tired. I thought, *Lord, I don't think I've got enough energy*—oomph—*to make it back to the surface.* At that point, out of my whole life, I can honestly say I

---

[2] He is my loving husband. I thank God for him every day.

gave up. I hate to admit it. I went as far as I could go physically and mentally. It was just me and the good Lord. In my mind, I was thinking, *Lord, I am so sorry that I am giving up. If there's any way you could let momma know, I did my best.*

At that point in time, it was as if you would have taken a movie camera of my whole life and hit fast rewind—my whole life replayed in its entirety. It was just at that point in time that an arm reached down and grabbed me by the shirt and pulled me up. I remember as the water came out of my ears I heard, "Are you okay?" And I said, "Yeah, man, I'm good." I didn't even take a deep breath, but I just felt good! I said, "Thank you, VanTassel." He looked over at me like okay. He looked at me kind of weird, a look that didn't fit. I can tell you I felt like a 115 horse-powered Evinrude! I started paddling and felt good! We finally made it to the bank of the river. VanTassel kept looking at me strangely. I felt so good. I didn't hurt, and I was completely energized.

Six months later, I was reliving the mission and all that took place at the river (even though you are supposed to forget the mission so you can keep moving forward to the next mission). Some of the pieces did not fit. Several years later, VanTassel verified what took place during that mission. He said he took the weapons from me. I was carrying mine and Willie Henry's weapon, and then I lay back in the water and disappeared way below the surface of the water. I asked him if I was right beside him, and he said, "No, you weren't." He recalled, "You were out of our sight." And he stated that I was under the water for about eight to ten minutes. They moved about twenty-five yards and that I had come up right beside them. He said he did not reach down and grab me and pull me up out of the water. I asked him, "Well, whose arm reached down and grabbed me?"

The more I thought about it, after several more years of recollecting the event, the more I recall that I did not see a chocolate-chip-colored BDU camouflaged jacket reach for me. It was a white robe with a light, as bright as the sun, that I saw as I was coming up and broke the surface of the water. I remember I had the most peaceful feeling. It was bright light, but I could look at it. It was pleasing to the eye. VanTassel said he didn't even touch me. As I broke the surface of the water, I also recollect hearing, "It's not your day" instead of "Are you okay?" It took ten years for all the pieces to fit together about that mission and for me realize that *it was not my day.*

Whether it was Jesus, or one of His angels, or God himself—I was pulled out of the water because I prayed to Him for help. I told Him I did my best and to let Momma know because that was all I could do. VanTassel verified to me that neither he nor any of the guys close to the raft reached down and grabbed me, and he also verified to me that I did go out of their sight as they moved twenty-five yards down the river. The fact that I came up and didn't even take a deep breath just amazes me! I prayed to Jesus, and he reached down and pulled me up out of a watery grave when I did not have the strength on my own to do so.

Collection of Favorites

Things learned:

1. Only God can create the joy and fulfillment through the Holy Spirit within us.
2. God does hear our prayers, and He answers our prayers according to his will.
3. The Bible is the true Word of God. It is the living Word of God.
4. Our body of armor protects us daily (Ephesians 6:11).
5. *Praise* is the ability to express approval (verbally), applaud, or to express adoration as in song. Praise is from the mouth.
6. *Worship* is giving praise, thanksgiving, and reverence from the heart. Worship is the praise that comes from the depths of our hearts and our minds. Worship is the act or feeling of adoration; love or admiration which comes from the heart.

Favorite Bible verses or sayings:

1. "They were all filled with the Holy Spirit and began to speak The word of God with boldness." (Acts 4:31)
2. "The man who was trying to trip Jesus up said to unto Him which is the greatest commandment? And Jesus

said unto him, 'Thou shalt love the Lord thy God with all thy heart, and with all thy soul, and with all thy mind.'" (Matthew 22:37)

3. "For God so loved the world, that He gave his only begotten Son, that whoever believes in Him shall not perish, but have eternal life." (John 3:16)

4. "Jesus said unto them, saying 'I am the light of the world, he that followeth me shall not walk in darkness, but shall have the light of life.'" (John 8:12)

5. "Jesus said to him, I am the way, and the truth, and the life; no one comes to the Father but through Me." (John 14:6)

6. "Finally brethren, whatever is true, whatever is honorable, whatever is right, whatever is pure, whatever is lovely, whatever is of good repute, if there is any excellence and if anything worthy of praise, dwell on these things. The things you have learned and received and heard and seen in me, practice these things, and the God of peace will be with you." (Philippians 4:8–9)

7. "Delight yourself in the Lord; and he will give you the desires of your heart. Commit your way to the Lord, trust also in Him, and He will do it." (Psalm 37:4–5)

8. "It is better to take refuge in the Lord than to trust in man." (Psalm 118:8)

9. "For all have sinned and fallen short of the glory of God." (Romans 3:23)

10. "And we know that God causes all things to work together for good to those who love God, to those who are called according to His purpose." (Romans 8:28)

11. "For whosoever shall call upon the name of the Lord shall be saved." (Romans 10:13)

12. "Rejoice always; pray without ceasing; *in everything give thanks*; for this is God's will for you in Christ Jesus. Do not quench the Spirit; do not despise prophetic utterances. But examine everything carefully; hold fast to that which is good; abstain from every form of evil." (1 Thessalonians 5:16–19, italics added)

13. "For God hath not given us a spirit of fear; but of power, and of love, and of a sound mind." (2 Timothy 1:7)

14. "It's not about the results, it's about the obedience!" (As heard from Mr. Joe Handy at Crowville Baptist Church)

15. "Go out and *be* the church." (Brother Joe Senn)

Putting on the Full Armor of God

In order to do battle against the evil forces, we have to "take up the full armor of God" (Ephesians 6:13). The full armor consists of the following (indicating we need to arm ourselves and be alert and ready for battle):

1. *Belt of truth.* Girding up or putting on the belt of truth was a matter of pulling up all the loose ends in preparation for battle. The belt that pulls all the spiritual loose ends in is "truth."

2. *Breastplate of righteousness.* The breastplate was a sleeveless piece of leather covering the whole torso, protecting the heart and other vital organs. Righteousness or holiness is such a distinctive characteristic of God himself; it is a Christian's chief defense against the evil one. As believers faithfully live in obedience to and communion with Jesus Christ, righteousness or holiness produces in them the practical daily righteousness that becomes their spiritual breastplate.

3. *Shoes ready with the Gospel of peace.* Always have your feet ready to move with sharing the Word of God. The Gospel of peace pertains to the good news that, through Christ, believers are at peace with God

and that He is on their side (Romans 5: 6–10). It is that confidence of divine support that allows the believer to stand firm, knowing that since he is at peace with God, God is his strength (Romans 8:31, 37–39).

4. *Shield of faith.* This is the believer's shield to extinguish all fiery arrows of the devil. The Romans had this huge shield that protected the whole body. Our faith in Jesus Christ protects the believer and all his family. This refers to a basic trust in God. The believer's continual trust in God's Word and promises protect the believer(s) from all temptations and sin. All sin comes when the victim falls to Satan's lies and promises of pleasure while rejecting the better choice of obedience and blessing (the *McArthur Study Bible,* p. 1785).

5. *Helmet of salvation.* This is having no doubt of your salvation through Jesus Christ. Satan seeks to destroy a believer's assurance of salvation with his weapons of doubt and discouragement (p. 1785), but the Christian can be strong in God's promises of eternal salvation as noted in scripture: John 6:37–39, 10:28–29; Romans 5:10, 8:31–39; Philippians 1:6; 1 Peter 1:3–5.

6. *Sword of the Spirit.* As the Roman soldier's only weapon was his sword, so the Word of God is the only weapon we believers need. The Word of God is the Bible. Our sword—our defensive and offensive tool, the sword of the Spirit—is the holy Word. Written by men and inspired by the Holy Spirit. It is our guide. It is the living Word of God.

Weapons against Evil

Our weapons are against satanic forces not fleshly. "For though we walk in the flesh, we do not war according to the flesh, for the weapons of our warfare are not of the flesh" (2 Corinthians 10:3–4). Our *weapons* of warfare are the following (inspired from the Holy Spirit in sermon given on August 30, 2015 by Brother Joe Senn):

1. *Faith* overcomes the world. "For by grace you have been saved through *faith*; and that not of yourselves, it is the gift of God; not as a result of works, so that no one may boast" (Ephesians 2:8, italics added).
2. *Praise.* "This is an honor for all His Godly ones. Praise the Lord!" (Psalm 149:9). "Let everything that has breath praise the Lord!" (Psalm 150:6) Praise the Lord!
3. *Prayer.* "And all things you ask in prayer, believing, you will receive" (Matthew 21:22).

Afterword

This book and these testimonies are written to help you "see" with your heart the works of the Lord. My life has been affected by my spiritual growth and my journey. May your life be affected as well. This is my attempt to help gather the lost sheep—in His name for His glory! I plant the seed of faith; it is *His* job to water the seed and make it grow. May we all be able to gather upon the green pasture on the other side.

The Bible is a book that does bring great *joy* into your life, especially if you become familiar with it, if you learn more about the stories, and it becomes your friend rather than just a doorstop gathering dust. So to my Aunt Evon and Uncle Frank, thank you for the greatest gift anyone could ever give—my Bible is a treasure. Thirty years later, and I still do find the joy and peace you spoke about way back when I was just sixteen.

To you, the person holding this book: I love you, I love you, and I love you. Do great things, be filled with His love and Joy. Create a legacy for yourself. Live life knowing that Heaven awaits us and that there is hope for the future!

Warmly yours, and in His obedience. May his mercy and love be upon you all the days of your life, in Jesus Christ's holy name I pray, Amen.

Remember this, it is not about being *religious*, it is a heart thing. God is love. Having a relationship with Christ is a relationship thing! Test it out- have faith, ask Him first when you are in need and see what HE can do.

If you would like to add your testimony of faith to my next book, please send your e-mail to me right away at Teresa8870@outlook.com and put in the subject "Testimony." Your testimony may touch the heart of someone and plant the seed of faith. Praise be to God the glory.

Prayer of Salvation

Father, I know I am a sinner because we have all sinned and fallen short of the glory of God. I am asking for Your forgiveness of my sins. Father, I know You are the way to eternal life. Lord, I confess with my mouth and believe in my heart that God raised Jesus from the dead. Father, I call upon your holy name to save me. Father, send your Holy Spirit to live within me so I may live my life for You. Thank you, Lord, for saving me and for Your grace and mercy. Amen.

Jesus spake unto them saying, "I am the light of
the world, he that followeth me shall not walk
in darkness, but shall have the light of life."
—2 Timothy 1:7

Rejoice with me, for I have found my sheep which was lost!
—Luke 15:6

Works Cited

1. MacArtur, John. The MacArthur Study Bible. New American Standard Bible Updated Edition. Thomas Nelson, 2006.

2. McVea, Crystal and Tresniowski, Alex. Waking up in Heaven. Howard Books, A division of Simon & Schuster, Inc. 2013.

3. Permissions have been granted to add testimonials which have been given for the purposes of being included in *Gather Ye Sheep.*

4. Virkler, Mark and Patti. How to Hear God's Voice. Destiny Image Publishers, 2005. "Reproduced by permission of Mark and Patti Virkler."

Printed in the United States
By Bookmasters